VIOLET LOVES THE LETTER V: VIRGIN ISLANDS PRIDE

WRITTEN BY INGRID A. BOUGH

ILLUSTRATED BY STUART P. RAMES

Outskirts Press, Inc.
http://www.outskirtspress.com

Paperback ISBN: 978-1-4787-8413-5
Hardback ISBN: 978-1-9772-1664-9

Library of Congress Control Number: 2019909629

Illustrations © 2019 Stuart P. Rames. All rights reserved - used with permission.

Outskirts Press and the "OP" logo are trademarks belonging to Outskirts Press, Inc.

PRINTED IN THE UNITED STATES OF AMERICA

This book is dedicated in the memory of my mother Violet A. Bough who wanted to be remembered as an educator, historian, church organist, and culture bearer.

Her dedication to her beloved homeland, years of service and contributions in the VI Department of Education, and to the entire Virgin Islands community will always be remembered.

Violet loves the color violet which is a shade of purple. Her father tells her that purple is the color of royalty. Violet's favorite flowers are violets which grow on her island.

Today, she will play a word game and try to create a story with as many people, places and things that begin with the letter V. Can you help her?

Violet lives in the town of Frederiksted on St. Croix in the United States Virgin Islands. The four inhabited islands are St. Croix, St. Thomas, St. John and Water Island. The islands are in surrounded by the Caribbean Sea and the Atlantic Ocean.

Some people confuse the British Virgin Islands with the U.S. Virgin Islands. They are located very close to each other, but belong to different countries. Jost Van Dyke is in the BVI. The U.S. Virgin Islands is one of the United States territories. These islands are very close to a larger island, Puerto Rico, which is a commonwealth of the United States.

Violet's father told her that the ancestors that were brought to the islands a very long time ago, travelling on ships which made long voyages from Africa.

Violet likes to look through the large window in her house because she can see the pier in her town. Vessels that travel from faraway places bring visitors to the islands. Violet likes to walk around the vendor booths near the pier. Some vendors sell local arts & crafts, and others sell fruits like mangoes, sugar apples, guavas, soursop, coconuts, and vegetables that grow on the island.

Many islanders are vegan. Do you know the difference between a vegan and a vegetarian? A vegan is a person who does not eat or use animal products. Some vegetarians eat dairy products and eggs and also use animal products, such as leather and fur.

Velkommen means
WELCOME in Danish!

Violet remembers seeing that red and white
flag sign at the airport and on the pier. The flag
is for the country of Denmark. Many visitors to
the islands are from the country of Denmark. They
are known as Danes and the official language is Danish.
There are Danish descendants that live on the island.

The year 2017 was a special year because it marked 100 years
since the Danish West Indies were sold from Denmark to the
United States (1917-2017) for $25,000,000 in gold.

The 31st of March is recognized every year as "Transfer
Day" in the United States Virgin Islands. This day
commemorates the official transfer of the islands
which took place in 1917. It was at this "transfer
day" that the islands became *The Virgin
Islands of the United States
of America."

Violet's friends Valencia and Vincente play on the volleyball team at their school. The twins were born on the small island of Vieques, located between Puerto Rico and St. Thomas. Vieques and the neighboring island of Culebra are not Virgin Islands, they do not share in the history and culture of their neighbor islands. Vieques and Culebra are part of Puerto Rico.

One day Violet hopes when her family goes on vacation they visit places that start with the letter V like the Vatican City, Venice in Italy, Venezuela, St. Vincent, or Vanuatu. So many places that start with a V, what is a girl to do?

On St. Croix, Violet loves to visit the Mount Victory Camp in the rainforest. On the way to the camp, there many tree vines hanging in the forest, fruit trees, birds and mongoose. Beware of venomous spiders and centipedes! Late at night under the tents on Halloween, ghost stories are told locally known as jumbie stories on the island. Some of the stories are very scary and make all the children scream!

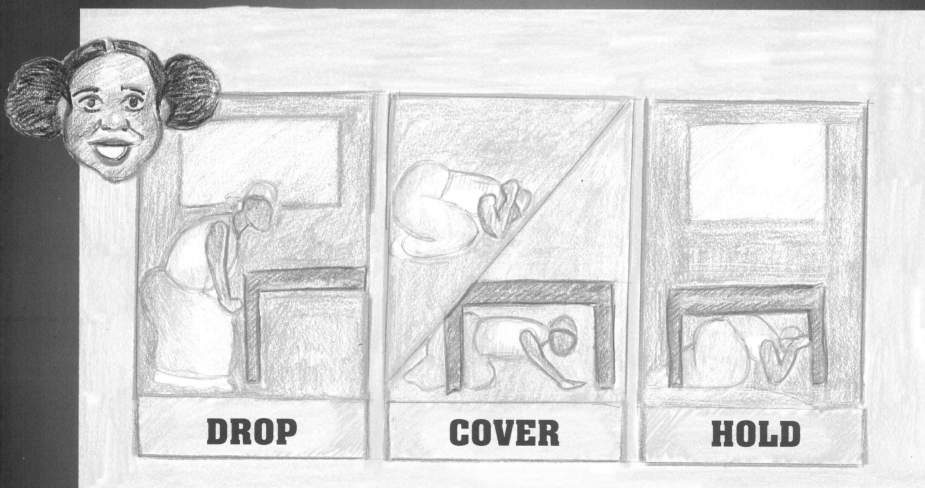

There are no volcanos on these islands. Sometimes, late at night while sleeping in the tents, you can feel small tremors from small earthquakes that makes the earth vibrate. This is scary feeling because on an island surrounded by water, there are not a lot of places to hide if there was ever a very big earthquake.

When an earthquake starts, Violet's
mother and father tell her to be brave
like her grandfather, a veteran
who served in World War II.

Violet's grandfather keeps his old military uniform
medals and ribbons in a very special place.

Just like her grandfather, Violet loves music!
Her grandfather used to play a violin.
Now that he is very old, he gave it her,
so she that she can learn to play.

Sometimes, Violet confuses the word veteran and veterinarian which is where her mother takes their dog, Van-Gogh. Her mother says, "Van-Gogh" is the name of a very famous Dutch painter Vincent van-Gogh.

The veterinarian always tells us to give Van-Gogh doggie vitamins, so he can stay healthy and strong.

Violet takes children's vitamins to stay healthy
and strong. One day, Violet saw a small glass on the
kitchen counter next to her vitamins. She thought it
was apple juice to drink with her vitamins.
YUCK!!! UGH! It was vinegar!

Her mother laughed and laughed! Spitting out the vinegar
which left a bad taste in her mouth, Violet was happy her
mother gave her a big bowl of her favorite locally made
Armstrong Homemade vanilla ice cream.

During the Christmas festival season, Violet's grandmother bakes a red velvet cake and a delicious Crucian Vienna cake. The Crucian Vienna cake is a very special cake with many delicious ingredients. Violet cannot decide which one she likes best.

Another special day is Valentine's Day! Violet loves spending time with her grandmother. They have fun drawing special heart shaped cards for friends and family.

They also bake heart shaped sugar cookies and Violet puts a candied V in the middle of the delicious cookies, so everyone knows the cookies are from Violet with LOVE who loves the letter V.

After the Christmas holidays on St. Croix, there is a festival around the holiday known as "Three Kings Day". There is a parade for children and a parade for adults.

Violet can't wait to go to the parade to see all the colorful costumes, the majorettes and steelpan bands and especially the moko jumbies. Violet's mother says there will be many VIP's attending the parades like the Governor, the Lieutenant Governor, queens, princesses, and other dignitaries.

Violet knows that VIP also stands for Virgin Islands Pride. Violet takes pride that she is from such a unique place surrounded by the blue waters of the Caribbean Sea and the Atlantic Ocean. Violet thinks that she is a VIP because she is unique and one of kind, and that makes her a very important person.

Wow! It surely has been a very long day thinking about all those people, places and things that begin with the letter V. As the Violet settles down in her bed, Violet looks through her window overlooking the pier and sees the sunset on the horizon..... and suddenly...it vanishes (POOF!) The next day it rises vertically high in the sky.

Activity:
How many words
(people, places and things)
in this story have the letter V?

What other people, places and things can you think of in your home with the letter V?

CPSIA information can be obtained at www.ICGtesting.com
Printed in the USA
BVIW121828070819
555302BV00010B/50